EQAO Grade 3 Math Test Prep

—— Teacher Guide ——

Written by Ruth Solski

RUTH SOLSKI was an educator for 30 years. She has written many educational resources and is the founder of S&S Learning Materials. As a writer, her main goal is to provide teachers with a useful tool that they can implement in their classrooms to bring the joy of learning to children.

Copyright © On The Mark Press 2016

This publication may be reproduced under licence from Access Copyright, or with the express written permission of On The Mark Press, or as permitted by law. All rights are otherwise reserved, and no part of this publication may be reproduced, stored in a retrieval system, or transmitted in any form or by any means, electronic, mechanical, photocopying, scanning, recording or otherwise, except as specifically authorized.

All Rights Reserved.
Printed in Canada.

Published in Canada by:
On The Mark Press
15 Dairy Avenue, Napanee, Ontario, K7R 1M4
www.onthemarkpress.com

Funded by the Government of Canada

SSG112   ISBN: 9781487704018 © On The Mark Press

Table of Contents

TEST #1: Number Sense and Numeration 3

TEST #2: Patterning and Algebra 10

TEST #3: Measurement. 17

TEST #4: Geometry and Spatial Sense 24

TEST #5: Data Managements and Probability. . 31

TEST #6: Mixed Math Skills 38

TEST #7: Mixed Math Skills 46

TEST #8: Mixed Math Skills 54

TEST #9: Mixed Math Skills 62

TEST #10: Mixed Math Skills 70

ANSWER KEY. 78

About This Book

This book was created to help Grade 3 students prepare for the EQAO Mathematics Assessment test. The 10 practice tests were designed to be similar to the actual test the students will be taking. The questions are either multiple choice or open response so that students can get familiar with the question/answer format.

The first 5 tests each feature a different key math skill for targeted practice: Number Sense and Numeration, Patterning and Algebra, Measurement, Geometry and Spatial Sense, and Data Management and Probability. Students struggling in any of these areas will benefit from this skill-specific practice. The following 5 tests feature mixed math skills with questions that are a combination of all the math skills.

There is no particular sequence to the tests. They can be used in whatever order you choose to fit your students needs.

Test #1: Multiple Choice

Number Sense and Numeration

1. The animal shelter has a total of 286 cats and dogs. There are 157 dogs.

   How many cats are in the shelter?

   ○ 118
   ○ 129
   ○ 443
   ○ 97

2. Which series of numbers shows counting by 25s?

   ○ 25, 35, 50, 75
   ○ 50, 75, 100, 125
   ○ 100, 110, 120, 130
   ○ 25, 50, 100, 150

3. Which group of three numbers equals 17?

   ○ 5, 8, 4
   ○ 6, 2, 3
   ○ 9, 3, 7
   ○ 8, 7, 1

4. Which number sentence could you use to check the answer for the following number sentence?

   76 − 39 = 37

   ○ 39 + 76 = 115
   ○ 39 − 37 = 2
   ○ 37 + 39 = 76
   ○ 115 − 76 = 39

Test #1: Multiple Choice

Number Sense and Numeration

5. What value does the digit 6 represent in the number 693?

   ○ 6 ones
   ○ 6 tens
   ○ 6 hundreds
   ○ 6 thousands

6. How many more is 58 than 32?

   ○ 18
   ○ 25
   ○ 19
   ○ 26

7. Which group of numbers is arranged from least to greatest?

   ○ 5921 5725 6525
   ○ 2969 4434 3271
   ○ 2301 2310 2321
   ○ 5834 5661 5889

8. Which of the following sets of blocks represents the number 364?

   ○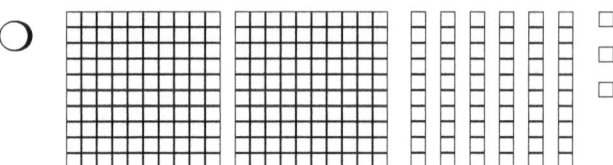

   ○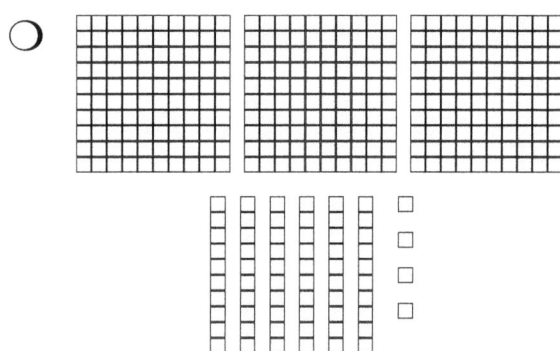

   ○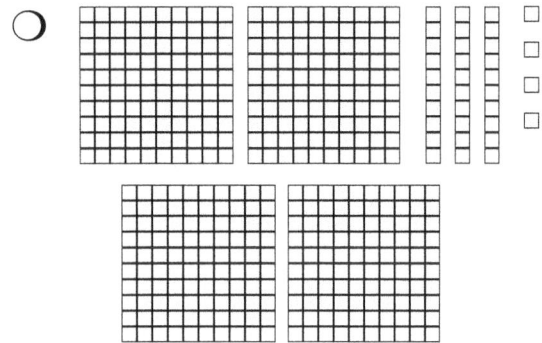

   ○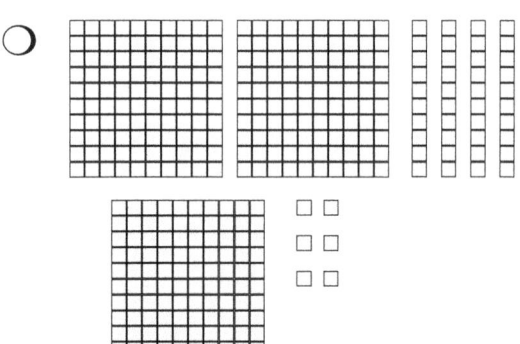

Test #1: Open Response

Number Sense and Numeration

9. A group of 68 tourists are gathered for a tour of Niagara Falls. There are 3 minibuses and 2 cars waiting to take them on the tour. Each minibus can carry 15 people. Each car can carry 5 people.

   How many people can leave for the tour right away?
   How many will have to wait for the next minibus?

   Show your work.

   _____ **tourists can leave right away.**

   _____ **tourists have to wait for the next minibus.**

Test #1: Open Response

Number Sense and Numeration

10. Jenny loves sweets! On Friday she had 15 tootsie rolls, and 12 pieces of licorice. Over the weekend she ate ⅔ of the tootsie rolls, and ½ of the pieces of licorice.

    How many total pieces of candy did Jenny have left on Monday?

    Show your work.

    Jenny had _____ pieces of candy left on Monday.

Test #1: Open Response

Number Sense and Numeration

11. Juan is taking the train to Toronto. There are 3 stops along the way. It takes 45 minutes to get to the first stop, 2 hours to get to the second stop, 1 ½ hours to get to the third stop and then another 45 minutes to get to Toronto.

   How many minutes will it take Juan to get to Toronto?

   Show your work.

   It will take Juan _____ minutes to get to Toronto.

Number Sense and Numeration

12. Which pair of numbers has the sum of 60?

    ○ 19 26

    ○ 49 11

    ○ 11 42

    ○ 13 38

13. What values do the 3 and 8 represent in the number 3468?

    ○ 3 hundreds and 8 tens

    ○ 3 tens and 8 ones

    ○ 3 thousands and 8 ones

    ○ 3 thousands and 8 tens

14. Which pair of numbers have a difference of $2.00?

    ○ $1.50 $0.50

    ○ $6.50 $3.00

    ○ $6.50 $3.50

    ○ $6.50 $4.50

15. Which number sentence correctly describes the following group of soccer balls?

    ○ 16 ÷ 4 = 4

    ○ 16 ÷ 2 = 8

    ○ 3 × 5 = 15

    ○ 16 × 2 = 32

16. What is the largest 4-digit number you can make from the 5 numbers shown below? Use each number only once.

    4 2 8 1 3

    ○ 4813

    ○ 8432

    ○ 8341

    ○ 4832

Test #1: Open Response

Number Sense and Numeration

17. Andrea charges $6.00 per hour to babysit. Each week she babysits for 3 hours on Friday night and 2 hours on Saturday night. Andrea wants to save $300 for a trip to New York.

   How many weeks will it take for Andrea to save enough money?

   Show your work.

   It will take Andrea _____ weeks to save enough for her trip.

Test #2: Multiple Choice

Patterning and Algebra

1. What is the next number in this series?

    2, 6, 16, 26, 36

   ○ 36
   ○ 63
   ○ 46
   ○ 47

2. Which number completes the following number sentence?

    14 + 8 = 38 − ☐

   ○ 14
   ○ 12
   ○ 16
   ○ 18

3. Which group of snowflakes shows counting by twos?

   ○ ❄❄❄❄ ❄❄❄❄❄ ❄❄❄❄❄❄
   ○ ❄❄ ❄❄❄❄❄ ❄❄❄❄❄❄❄
   ○ ❄❄❄❄ ❄❄❄❄❄❄ ❄❄❄❄❄❄❄❄
   ○ ❄❄ ❄❄❄❄❄❄ ❄❄❄❄❄❄❄❄

4. Which number sentence completes the pattern of number sentences below?

    3 × 1 + 1 = 4
    3 × 2 + 2 = 8
    3 × 3 + 3 = 12
    3 × 4 + 4 = 16
    3 × 5 + 5 = 20

   ○ 3 × 8 + 4 = 28
   ○ 3 × 7 + 3 = 24
   ○ 3 × 5 + 3 = 18
   ○ 3 × 6 + 6 = 24

Test #2: Fill in the Blanks

Patterning and Algebra

5. Complete the following number patterns.

   a. 8, 24, 40, _____ , _____ , _____

   b. 28, 24, 20, _____ , _____ , _____

   c. 84, 72, _____ , 48, 36, _____ , _____

6. Write in the numbers that complete the following number sentences.

   a. $18 \div 3 - \boxed{} = 4$

   b. $12 \times 4 + 8 = \boxed{}$

   c. $44 \div 4 + \boxed{} = 16$

7. What are the next three numbers in this model?

   0 4 5 0 4 5 6 0 4 5 6 7 0 4 5 6 7 _____ _____ _____

8. Continue the following patterns.

   a. X1, X2, X4, X8, _____ , _____ , _____ , _____

   b. 13, 16, 19, 22, _____ , _____ , _____ , _____

   c. BA, DC, FE, HG, _____ , _____ , _____ , _____

Patterning and Algebra

Test #2: Open Response

9. Ms. Hahn is adding a new flower bed to her garden. The arrangement of flowers below is the pattern for the flower bed.

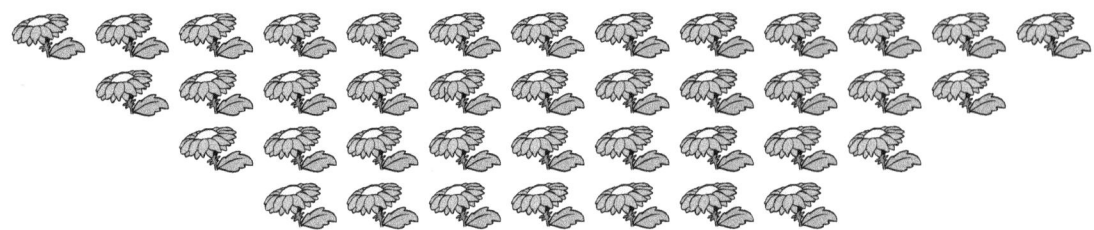

If she continues on with the same pattern, how many total flowers will there be in the next two rows?

Show your work. Explain your thinking.

There is a total of _____ flowers in the next two rows.

Test #2: Open Response

Patterning and Algebra

10. The rule "add 6" is used to shade in the numbers on the hundreds chart shown below. The pattern starts with the number 4.

   Continuing with the same rule, shade in the numbers on the rest of the chart.

1	2	3	**4**	5	6	7	8	9	**10**
11	12	13	14	15	**16**	17	18	19	20
21	**22**	23	24	25	26	27	**28**	29	30
31	32	33	**34**	35	36	37	38	39	**40**
41	42	43	44	45	**46**	47	48	49	50
51	52	53	54	55	56	57	58	59	60
61	62	63	64	65	66	67	68	69	70
71	72	73	74	75	76	77	78	79	80
81	82	83	84	85	86	87	88	89	90
91	92	93	94	95	96	97	98	99	100

a. The total of the shaded numbers in row 3 is _____ .

b. The total of the shaded numbers in row 7 is _____ .

c. The total of the shaded numbers in row 10 is _____ .

Patterning and Algebra

11. Lily is using a rule to make the number pattern below.

    358, 353, 348, 343

    Which of the following number patterns uses the same rule?

    ○ 655, 660, 665, 670
    ○ 618, 615, 612, 609
    ○ 629, 624, 619, 614
    ○ 639, 649, 659, 669

12. Shown below is a pattern using circles and squares.

    Which two attributes were used to make this pattern?

    ○ size and direction
    ○ shape and number
    ○ color and number
    ○ size and shape

13. Loren solves the following question.

    48 ÷ 6 = 8

    Which number sentence would help Loren check his answer?

    ○ 8 + 6 = 14
    ○ 48 − 6 = 42
    ○ 6 × 8 = 48
    ○ 8 × 48 = 384

14. Which of the following is an example of a repeating pattern?

    ○ taking a drive to the beach
    ○ going to the movies every Friday
    ○ having brunch on Sunday
    ○ reading a book

Patterning and Algebra

15. What three numbers are missing from the following pattern?

    365, 362, ___ , 356, 353, ___ , ___

    ○ 360, 350, 340
    ○ 361, 351, 350
    ○ 359, 350, 347
    ○ 359, 349, 339

16. Which number can be placed in the box to make this number sentence true?

    $243 + \boxed{} = 271$

    ○ 28
    ○ 18
    ○ 132
    ○ 101

17. Look at the number pattern below. What is the rule for this pattern?

    17, 21, 25, 29, 33

    ○ add 6
    ○ add 3
    ○ add 5
    ○ add 4

18. These two number sentences belong to the same fact family.

    $8 \times 4 = 32$ and $32 \div 8 = 4$

    Which of the following pair of number sentences belong to the same fact family?

    ○ $32 \times 4 = 128$ and $128 \div 4 = 32$
    ○ $4 \times 8 = 32$ and $32 \div 4 = 8$
    ○ $4 \times 4 = 16$ and $16 \times 16 = 32$
    ○ $8 \div 4 = 2$ and $2 \times 8 = 16$

Test #2: Open Response

Patterning and Algebra

19. Rick is teaching a class in skiing. He starts out with 3 students. Each day 3 new students show up for the class. The graph below shows how many students Rick has on Monday and Tuesday.

Fill in the graph with the total number of students for Wednesday, Thursday, and Friday to complete the graph.

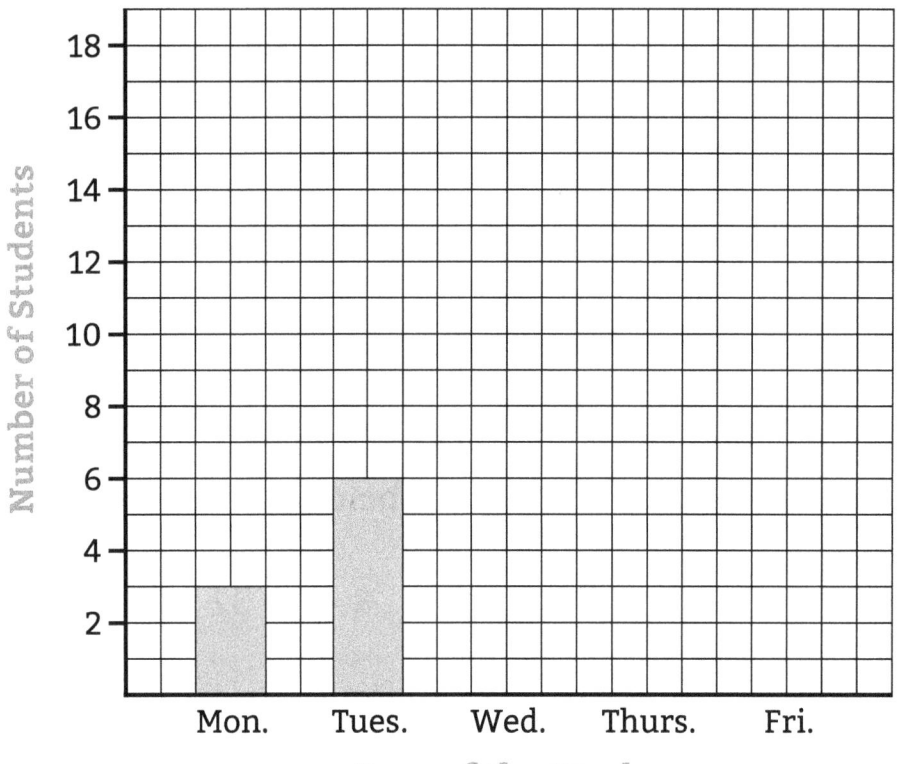

If 4 students go home early on Friday, _____ students will be left in the class.

Justify your answer.

Test #3: Multiple Choice

Measurement

1. Which clock shows 8:55?

   ○

   ○

   ○

   ○

2. When you are traveling in a car, which is the correct measurement unit to tell how fast you are going?

   ○ kilometre

   ○ kilogram

   ○ metre

   ○ centimetre

3. Which of the following thermometers shows 15°C?

   ○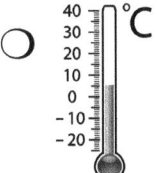

   ○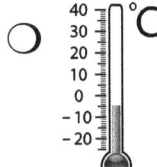

   ○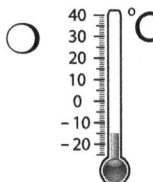

   ○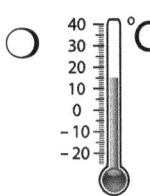

4. It will take 6 months to finish building the library.

   Which number is closest to how many days it will take to finish the library?

   ○ 170

   ○ 130

   ○ 180

   ○ 210

Measurement

Test #3: Multiple Choice

5. Which activity is most likely to be measured in minutes?

   ○ a school day
   ○ recess
   ○ a science project
   ○ a field trip

6. It's 5:55 and Mark has been working on his homework for the past 45 minutes.

   At what time did he start his homework?

   ○ 5:35
   ○ 5:10
   ○ 5:00
   ○ 5:05

7. Which combination of coins equals $5.53?

   ○

   ○

   ○

   ○

Test #3: Multiple Choice

Measurement

8. Which of the following sets of items can be measured in litres?

   ○ a bar of soap, a can of pop
   ○ a can of soup, a bag of rice
   ○ gasoline, milk
   ○ carrots, apples

9. Amrita was not feeling well and she had to stay in bed for 3 days.

   How many hours did Amrita have to stay in bed?

   ○ 48
   ○ 72
   ○ 60
   ○ 96

10. What time is shown on the clock below?

    ○ 10:15
    ○ 9: 20
    ○ 10:10
    ○ 10:20

11. Tony wants to drink at least 1 litre of water a day. He bought a case of bottled water to help him with his goal. Each bottle of water is 250 millilitres.

    How many bottles of water will Tony need to drink to equal 1 litre?

    ○ 3 bottles
    ○ 5 bottles
    ○ 4 bottles
    ○ 2 bottles

Measurement

12. If each side of a square measures 1 centimetre, what is the perimeter of figure A?

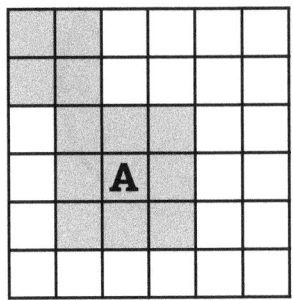

- ○ 14 cm
- ○ 18 cm
- ○ 19 cm
- ○ 17 cm

13. Using each shaded square as a unit of measurement, what is the area of figure B?

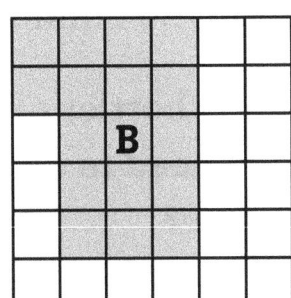

- ○ 17 squares
- ○ 20 squares
- ○ 16 squares
- ○ 18 squares

14. Amy has a litre bottle of apple juice. She and her brother drank some of the juice for breakfast. Figure A shows a full bottle of juice. Figure B shows how much juice was left after breakfast.

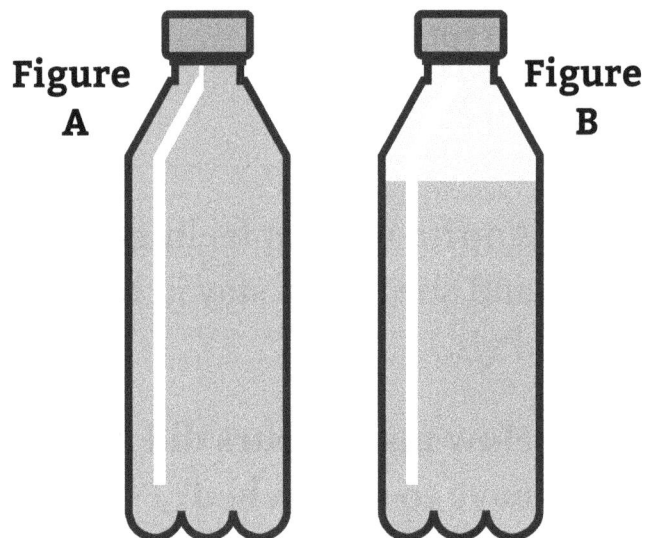

Approximately how much of the litre did Amy and her brother drink?

- ○ ½ litre
- ○ ¾ litre
- ○ ¼ litre
- ○ ⅔ litre

Measurement

Test #3: Open Response

15. Mr. Weaver's ranch has a fenced in pasture for his cattle and a fenced in pasture for his horses. The figures below show the size of each pasture.

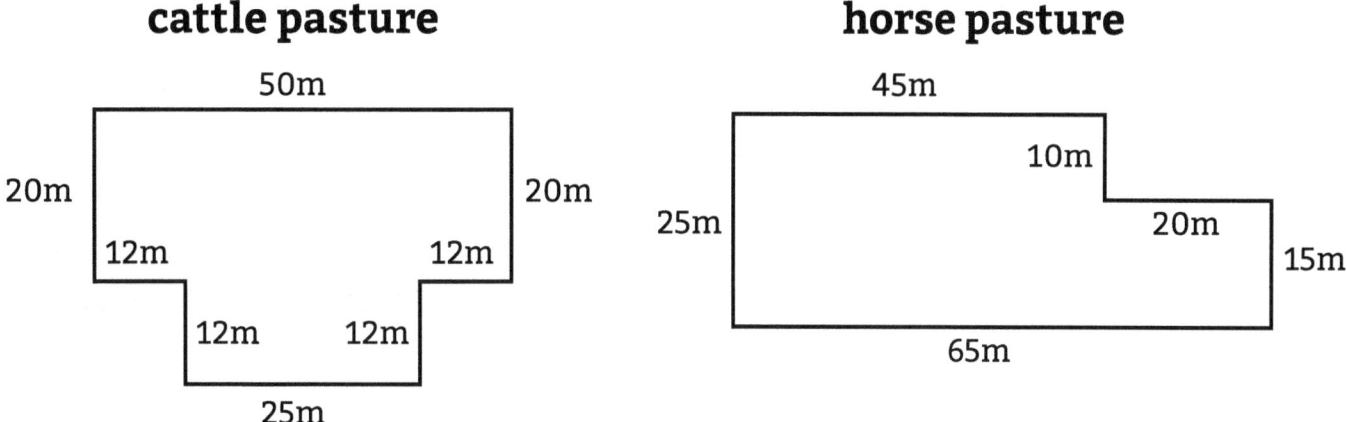

Which pasture has the largest perimeter?

Show your work.

The _____ pasture has the largest perimeter.

Test #3: Open Response

Measurement

16. Kamal's house is 4.5 metres high. The two story house next door is 6 metres high.

   How many decimetres higher is the house next door?
   How many centimetres higher?

   Show your work.

   The house next door is _____ decimetres higher
   or _____ centimetres.

Test #3: Open Response

Measurement

17. The zoo is expanding the space for the lions. Below are the two plans that are being considered. Each square is 1 m by 1 m.

Plan A **Plan B**

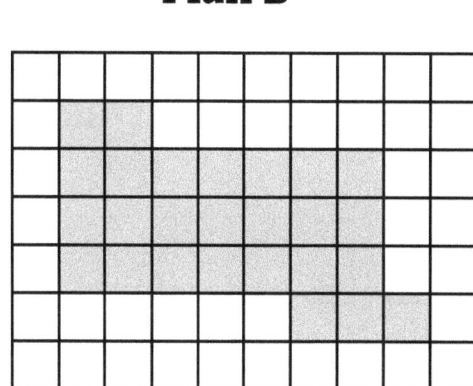

Which plan has the largest area for the lions?

Explain your answer.

_____ has the largest area for the lions.

Test #4: Multiple Choice

Geometry and Spatial Sense

1. Which geometric solid can be made from the following shapes?

   ○ cube
   ○ square-based pyramid
   ○ triangular prism
   ○ cylinder

2. How many sides are in the following shape?

   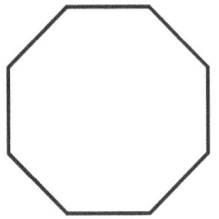

   ○ 6 sides
   ○ 9 sides
   ○ 8 sides
   ○ 10 sides

3. Which of the following shapes is a four-sided figure?

   ○ triangle
   ○ octagon
   ○ pentagon
   ○ rectangle

4. Identify the following geometric solid shape.

   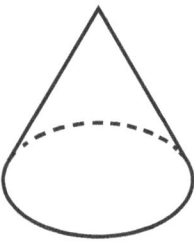

   ○ cone
   ○ pyramid
   ○ cylinder
   ○ cube

Test #4: Multiple Choice

Geometry and Spatial Sense

5. I am a geometric solid that can roll. What shape am I?

   ○ cube
   ○ cylinder
   ○ pyramid
   ○ prism

6. Which of these letters can be folded in half so that the parts are an exact match?

   ○ N
   ○ P
   ○ R
   ○ X

7. How many of Shape A can be found in Shape B?

   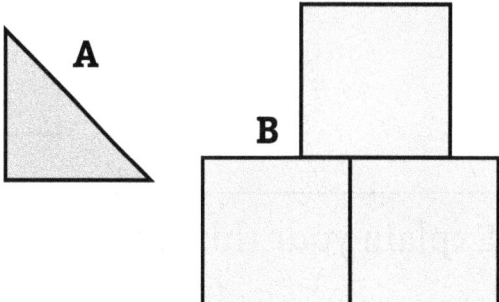

   ○ 6 shapes
   ○ 8 shapes
   ○ 4 shapes
   ○ 5 shapes

8. Which of the following shapes is a parallelogram?

   ○
   ○
   ○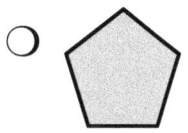
   ○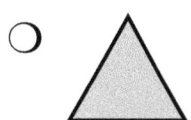

Geometry and Spatial Sense

9. A square has four lines of symmetry. Draw the four lines of symmetry in the squares below.

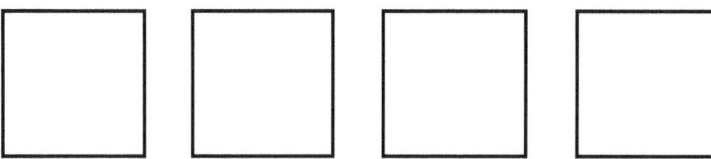

Explain your thinking.

10. Which of the following shapes are congruent?

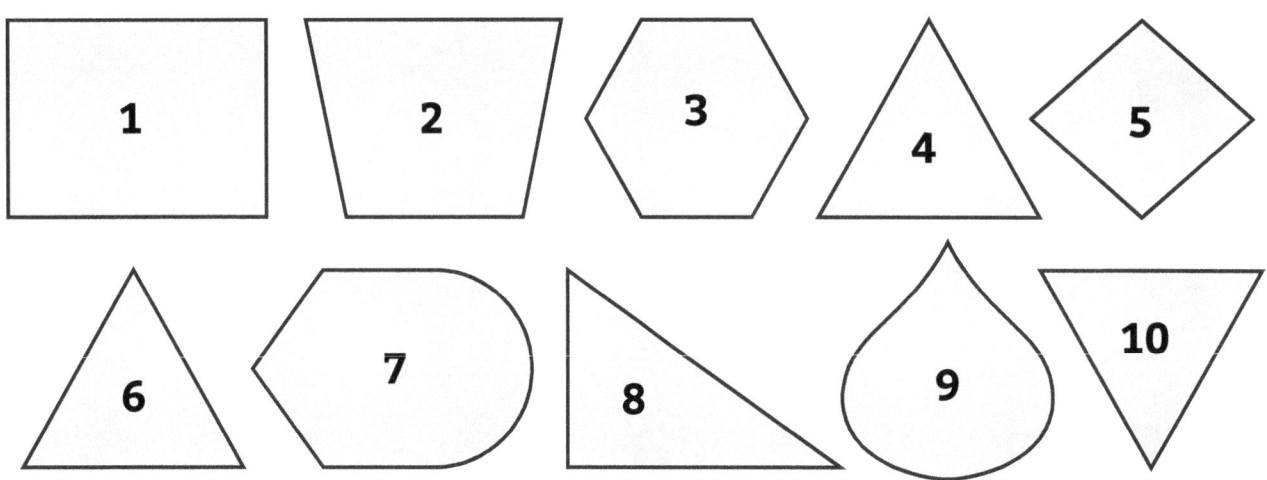

The congruent shape numbers are _____.

Test #4: Open Response

Geometry and Spatial Sense

11. The grid below shows a map of four fun places to visit. Each square on the grid represents 1 kilometre. A description of the route from Granite Falls to Water World is: 3 kilometres up and 4 kilometres to the left.

Four Fun Places to Visit

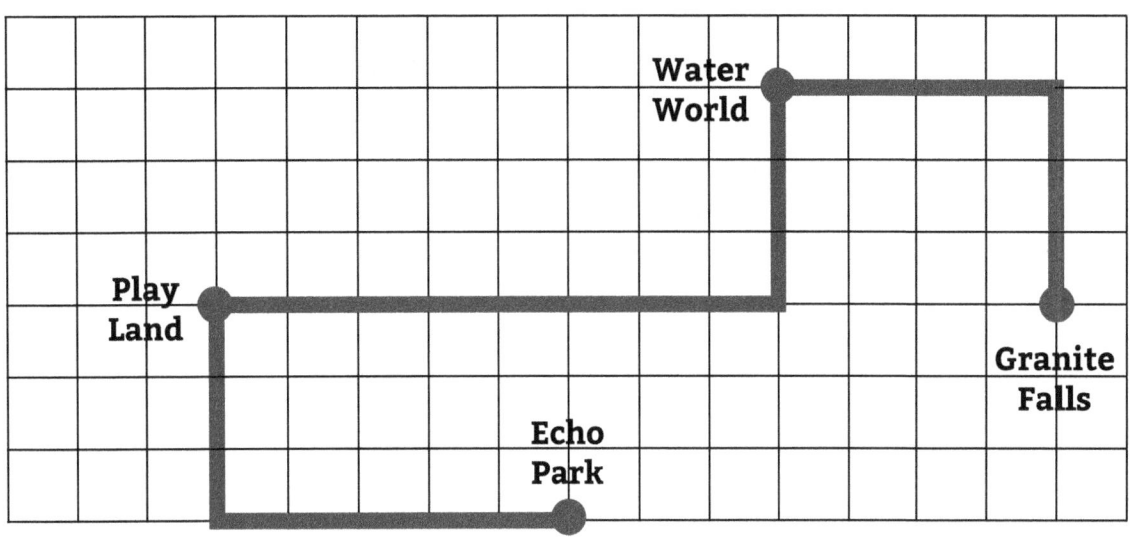

Describe a route from Water World to Play Land.

Describe a route from Play Land to Echo Park, then from Echo Park back to Water World.

Test #4: Open Response

Geometry and Spatial Sense

12. Classify the shapes below. Write the letter of each shape in the correct classification box.

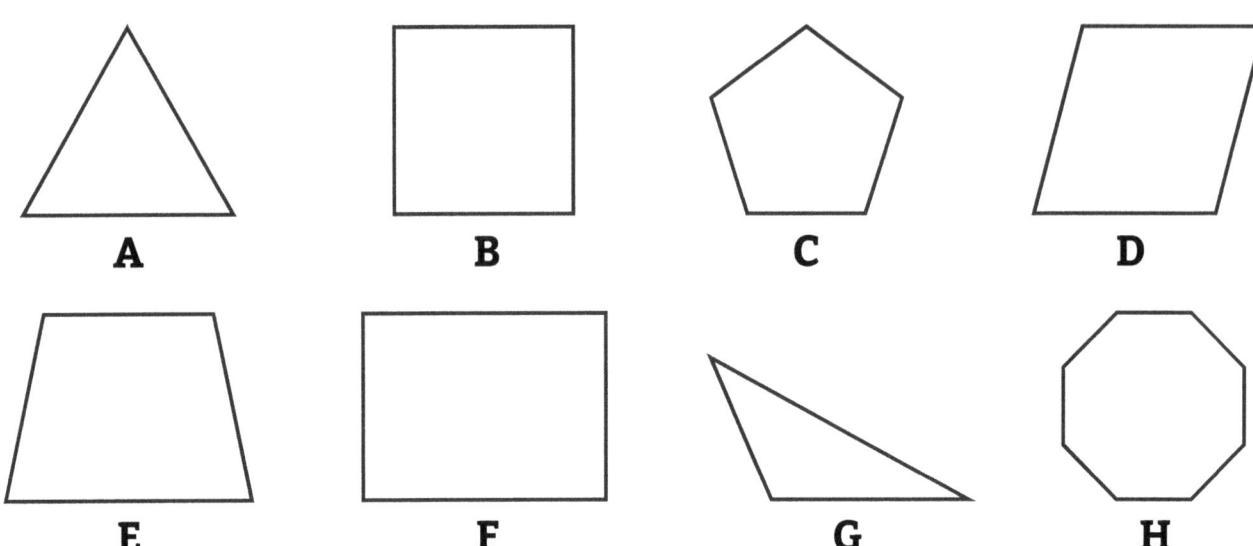

Shapes that are quadrilaterals.	Shapes that are *not* quadrilaterals.

Explain your answers.

Test #4: Open Response

Geometry and Spatial Sense

13. Complete the shape on the gird so that it is symmetrical. Use the dashed line as a line of symmetry.

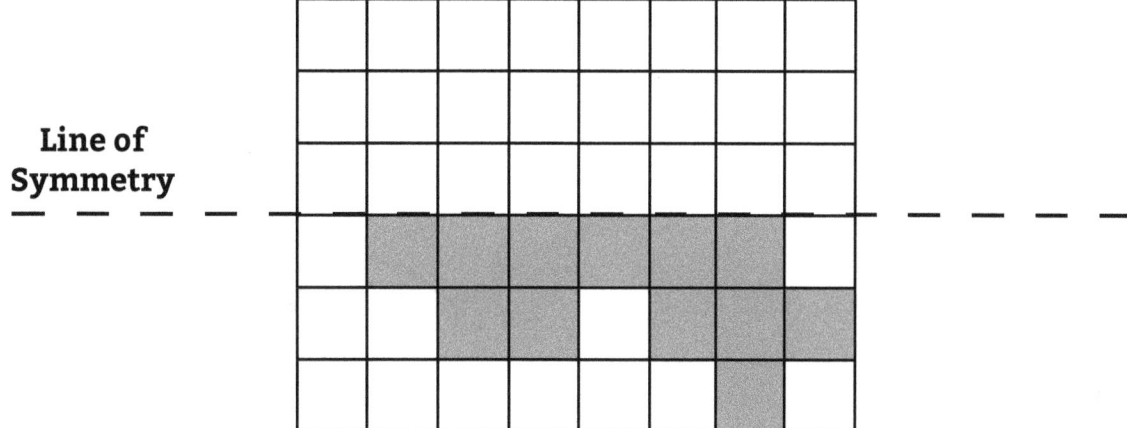

Explain how you know your completed shape is symmetrical.

14. The letter E in the figure below has gone through two transformations. Choose from the following words to describe each transformation: *rotation, reflection, translation*.

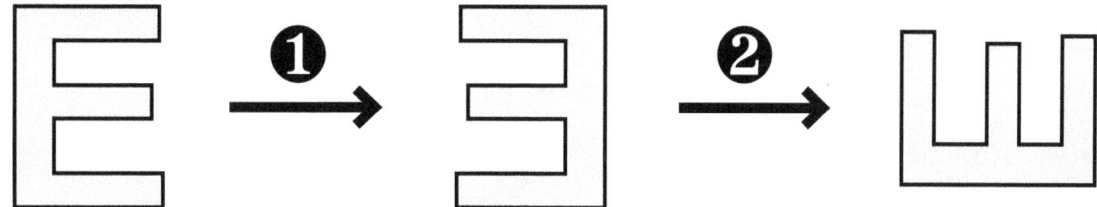

Transformation ❶: _____

Transformation ❷: _____

Geometry and Spatial Sense

Test #4: Multiple Choice

15. What is the total number of edges and vertices on the figure shown below?

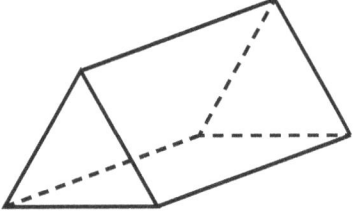

- ○ 5 edges, 5 vertices
- ○ 9 edges, 6 vertices
- ○ 6 edges, 9 vertices
- ○ 5 edges, 3 vertices

16. Which of the following shapes has only 1 line of symmetry?

 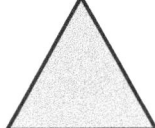

○

17. Which of the following shapes has 6 faces and right angles?

 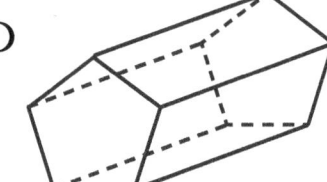

○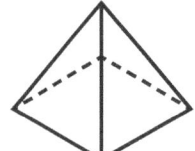

 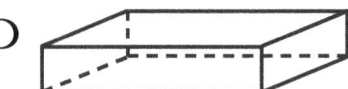

18. Which shape matches the following description?

All sides equal; two pairs of parallel lines; opposite angles equal.

- ○ octagon
- ○ triangle
- ○ rhombus
- ○ trapezoid

Data Management and Probability

1. Sunil placed 1 green apple, 1 red apple, 1 yellow apple and 1 striped apple into a basket. If Chan closes his eyes and picks an apple, what are his chances of getting a green apple?

   ○ 1 chance out of 4

   ○ 2 chances out of 3

   ○ 2 chances out of 4

   ○ 4 chances out of 4

2. Mrs. Munn's class did a survey of their favourite sports. The results are in the chart below.

Favourite Sports	
Hockey	11 students
Soccer	8 students
Basketball	7 students
Volleyball	6 students

   How many students were surveyed?

   ○ 15

   ○ 31

   ○ 29

   ○ 32

3. The Sweet Tooth Bakery made a chart to show how many of each dessert was sold daily.

Daily Desserts Sold	
Donuts	8
Cakes	4
Pies	8
Cookies	18
Brownies	12
Cupcakes	8
Fruit Tarts	4

   What number shows the mode of the bakery's data?

   ○ 12

   ○ 4

   ○ 8

   ○ 18

Data Management and Probability

4. Fill in the blanks with one of the following labels that best describes each event.

   impossible   unlikely   likely   certain

   a. I will eat some time today.   _____

   b. I will go to the moon one day.   _____

   c. It will rain this afternoon.   _____

   d. I will go to college.   _____

   e. A dinosaur will run through my back yard.   _____

   f. I will get dressed in the morning.   _____

5. The Bar S Ranch has the following animals in their barn: 8 brown horses, 3 white horses, and 1 donkey. Each Sunday friends come over to ride the animals.

   Fill in the blanks in the following sentences with the type of animal that best completes the sentence.

   a. It is most likely that a _____ will be ridden.

   b. It is unlikely that a _____ will be ridden.

   c. It is not possible for a _____ to be ridden.

   d. It is less likely that a _____ will be ridden.

Test #5: Open Response

Data Management and Probability

6. The chart below shows the results of Keisha spinning a spinner many times. It shows how many times the spinner landed on the flower image and how many times it landed on the star image.

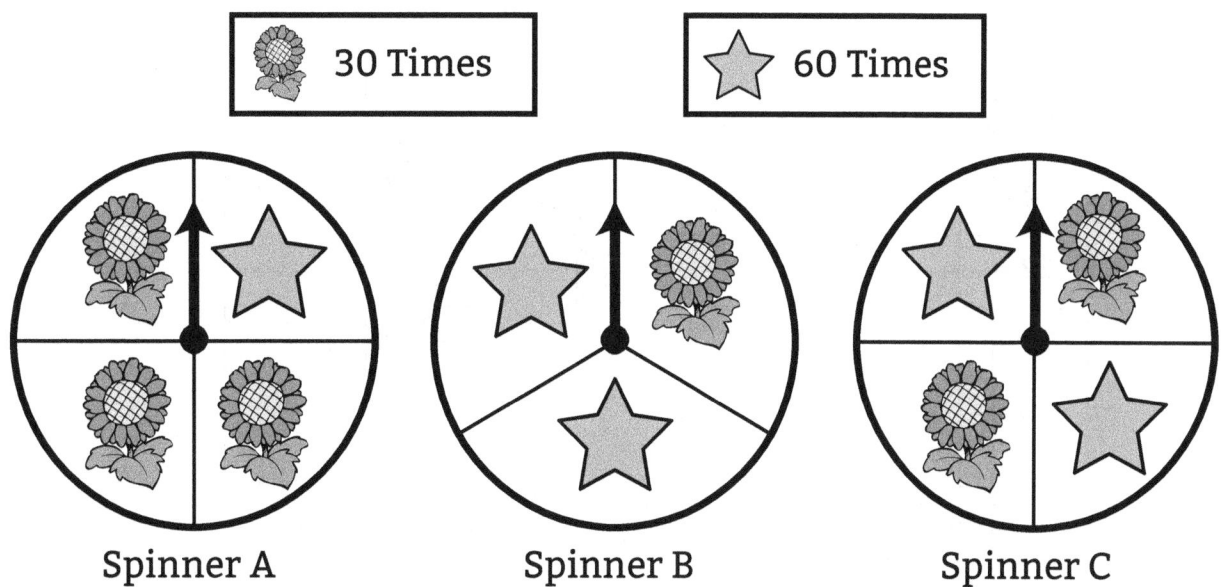

How many times did Keisha spin the spinner? _____

Which spinner did Keisha most likely use? _____

Explain your thinking.

Test #5: Open Response

Data Management and Probability

7. Mike finished reading his book last week. The graph below shows how many pages of his book he read each day of the week.

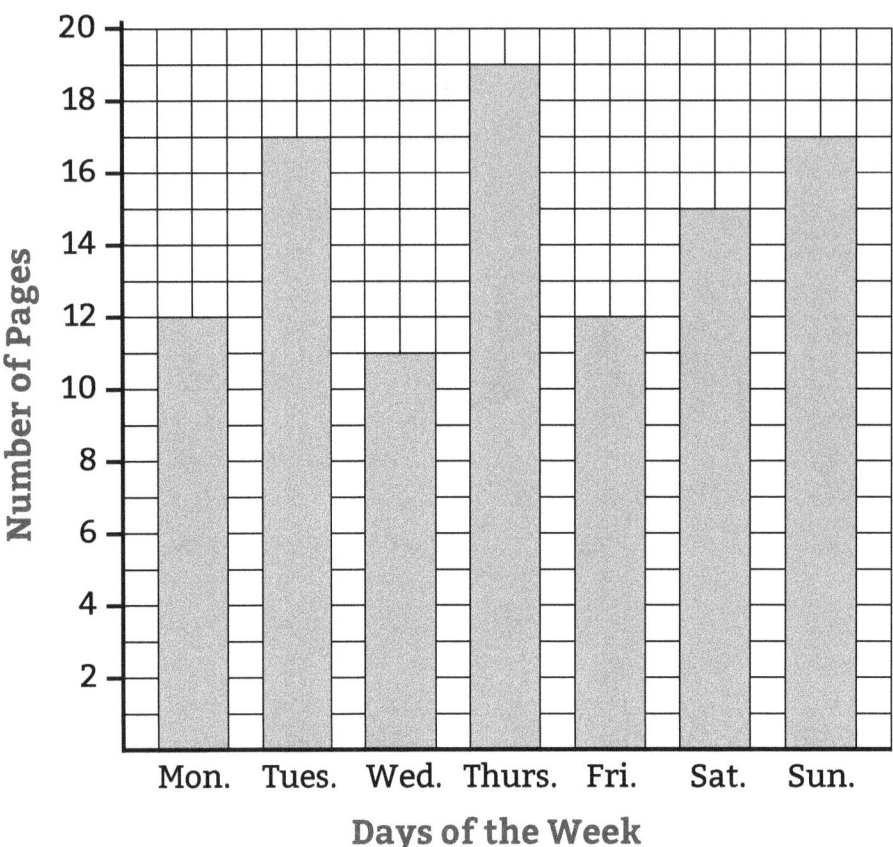

How many total pages did Mike read last week? _____

How many more pages did he read on Thursday than on Wednesday? _____

Mike's book is 220 pages long, how many pages had Mike read before last week? _____

Show your work.

Test #5: Open Response

Data Management and Probability

8. The movie studio wants to know what kind of movie to make next. They did a survey of 100 people to see what kind of movies are their favourite.

   The chart below shows the results of the survey.

Type of Movie	Number of People
Adventure	☺☺☺☺
Romance	
Comedy	☺☺☺☺☺☺
Drama	☺☺☺☺☺
Fantasy	☺☺

   Key: Each ☺ represents 5 people.

   The chart is missing the information for romance movies. Complete the chart to show how many people chose romance movies as their favourite.

   According to the chart, which kind of movie is the studio most likely to make next? _____

   Justify your answers.

Data Management and Probability

9. The number cube has 6 sides; each side has a number:

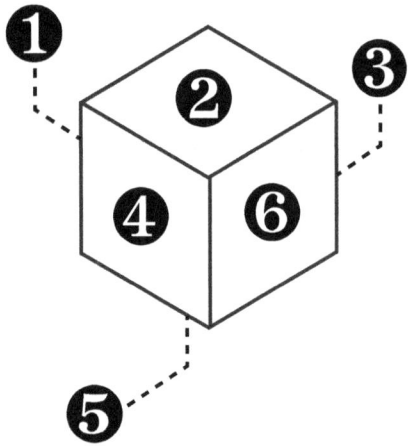

   If the number cube is rolled one time, what are the chances that the cube will land on the 1 or the 4?

   ○ 1 out of 4
   ○ 2 out of 6
   ○ 3 out of 4
   ○ 2 out of 5

10. Maria walked along the beach collecting rocks, seashells, and pieces of driftwood. She put 9 rocks, 4 seashells, and 2 small pieces of driftwood in her bucket. Maria asks her brother, Juan, to close his eyes and pick something from the bucket.

    Which word best describes the chance that Juan has of picking a rock?

    ○ impossible
    ○ unlikely
    ○ likely
    ○ certain

Data Management and Probability

Test #5: Multiple Choice

11. The channel 4 meteorologist made a graph of the weather for last month.

    Key: ✘ = 3 days

Type of Weather	Number of Days
Rainy	✘ ✘ ✘ ✘
Cloudy	✘ ✘
Sunny	✘ ✘ ✘
Partly Cloudy	✘

    Which of the following statements about the weather graph is true?

    ○ There were more sunny days than rainy days.

    ○ There was one more cloudy day than partly cloudy day.

    ○ There were fewer rainy days than cloudy days.

    ○ There were three more rainy days than sunny days.

12. Karina was organizing her closet and she decided to make a chart of what she found.

Karina's Closet	
T-Shirts	6
Skirts	4
Jeans	5
Pairs of Shoes	3
Dresses	4
Hats	3
Blouses	4

    Which number represents the mode of Karina's data?

    ○ 5

    ○ 4

    ○ 3

    ○ 6

Test #6: Multiple Choice

Mixed Math Skills

1. Which number sentence has the same answer as the number sentence below?

   3 x 5 + 5 =

   ○ 3 + 3 + 3 + 3 =
   ○ 2 x 5 + 20 =
   ○ 5 x 5 + 3 =
   ○ 5 + 5 + 5+ 5 =

2. Which number line is labelled correctly?

   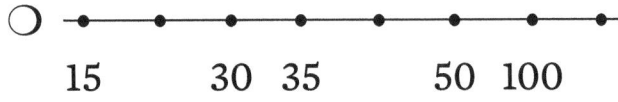
   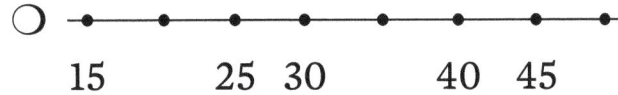
   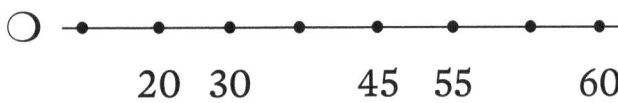
   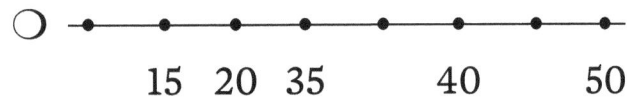

3. How many rectangles are in the following shape?

   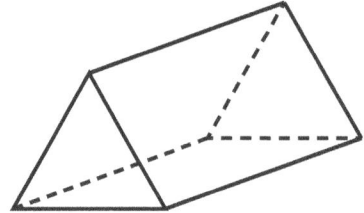

   ○ 3
   ○ 6
   ○ 4
   ○ 2

4. Luke lives on a large ranch. He has 320 sheep and 338 cows. How many more cows does he have?

   ○ 10 more cows
   ○ 12 more cows
   ○ 8 more cows
   ○ 18 more cows

Mixed Math Skills

Test #6: Multiple Choice

5. Kim has 2 different pairs of shorts and 2 different tee shirts. How many wardrobe combinations can she make?

   ○ one combination
   ○ four combinations
   ○ three combinations
   ○ two combinations

6. Look at the following number pattern.

   6, 10, 14, 18, 22, . . .

   If this pattern continues, what will the next three numbers be?

   ○ 28, 32, 40,
   ○ 23, 24, 25
   ○ 26, 30, 34
   ○ 24, 28, 32

7. What geometric solid can you make out of the following shapes?

   ○ sphere
   ○ cube
   ○ cone
   ○ square-based pyramid

8. Which number completes the following number sentence?

   $32 - 8 = \boxed{} + 6$

   ○ 18
   ○ 22
   ○ 13
   ○ 12

Test #6: Multiple Choice

Mixed Math Skills

9. Jaime is buying the snacks shown below.

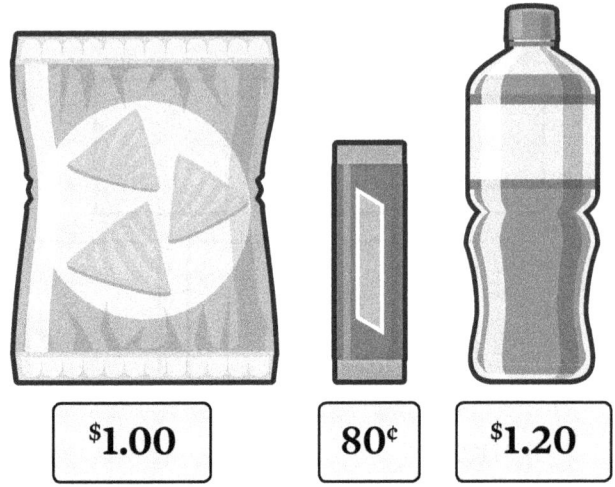

Jaime pays with a five-dollar bill. How much change will he receive?

○ $3.20

○ $2.40

○ $3.00

○ $2.00

10. How many lines of symmetry can be drawn on the following figure?

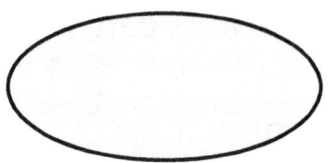

○ 1 line of symmetry

○ 4 lines of symmetry

○ 3 lines of symmetry

○ 2 lines of symmetry

11. Which clock shows 7:45?

○

○

○

○

Test #6: Open Response

Mixed Math Skills

12. The pet store had 18 goldfish on Friday. They sold 1/3 of the goldfish on Saturday and 3 more on Sunday. The goldfish sold for $3.00 each.

   How many goldfish were left on Monday?

   How much money did the store make on the goldfish they sold?

Show your work.

There were _____ goldfish left on Monday.

The store made _____ on the goldfish they sold.

Mixed Math Skills

13. Mr. Raman created a chart to represent the number of students in his class that had birthdays in each month of the year. Using that chart, shown below, create a bar graph that represents the information.

Months	Students
Jan.	4
Feb.	0
Mar.	4
Apr.	3
May.	5
Jun.	3
Jul.	1
Aug.	2
Sept.	2
Oct.	3
Nov.	2
Dec.	1

6												
5												
4												
3												
2												
1												
	J	**F**	**M**	**A**	**M**	**J**	**J**	**A**	**S**	**O**	**N**	**D**

How many students are in Mr. Raman's class? __________

How many more students have birthdays in May than in December? __________

Which months have an odd number of students?

____

____

SSG112 ISBN: 9781487704018

Mixed Math Skills

Test #6: Multiple Choice

14. Kali has a bag of colourful marbles. Each marble is a different colour. The colours are: teal, pink, orange, purple, green, yellow, black, and brown.

    If Kali asks her friend to pick a marble from the bag, what are the chances that she will get either a pink, green, or yellow?

    ○ 3 out of 6
    ○ 2 out of 5
    ○ 3 out of 8
    ○ 2 out of 8

15. Look at the two shapes below.

    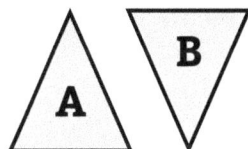

    How is it possible for A to become B?

    ○ Rotation
    ○ Reflection
    ○ Translation
    ○ A cannot become B

16. What unit of measure would you use to measure the length of an ink pen?

    ○ decimetre
    ○ metre
    ○ kilometre
    ○ centimetre

17. It's a very cold, snowy day in Toronto. Which of the following might be the temperature?

    ○ -3°C
    ○ 25° C
    ○ 14° C
    ○ 10° C

Test #6: Open Response

Mixed Math Skills

18. Malia used the graph below to plan out her vegetable garden. Which is the greater number, the perimeter of the garden or the area of the garden?

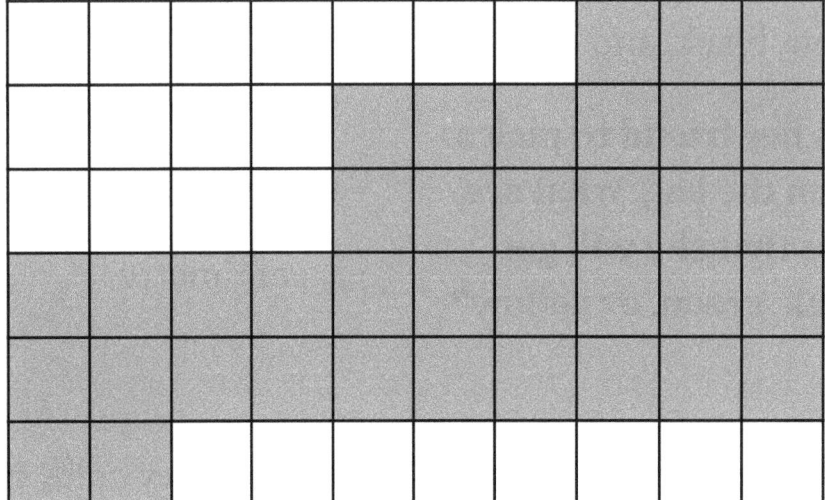

Show your work. Explain your thinking.

The perimeter is _____. The area is _____.

The _____ is the greater number.

Test #6: Open Response

Mixed Math Skills

19. The store sells the same number of lottery tickets each day.

    On Day 1 the store starts out with 118 tickets.

    On Day 2 the store has 113 tickets.

    On what day will the store have exactly 93 tickets left?

    Show your work.

    The store will have exactly 93 tickets left on Day _____.

20. Ben, Colin, and Marsha all put in the same amount to buy a video game that cost $36.00.

    How much did each person pay for the game?

    Show your work.

    Each person paid _____.

Mixed Math Skills

Test #7: Multiple Choice

1. Look at the number pattern below. What is the rule for this pattern?

   72, 69, 66, 63, 60, 57

   ○ subtract 2

   ○ add 4

   ○ add 3

   ○ subtract 3

2. The following fact family is missing one number sentence.

   9 x 3 = 27

   27 ÷ 3 = 9

   ?

   3 x 9 = 27

   Which of the following is the missing number sentence?

   ○ 3 x 3 = 9

   ○ 27 ÷ 9 = 3

   ○ 9 x 9 = 81

   ○ 9 ÷ 3 = 3

3. Which of the following looks like a cylinder?

   ○ a box of cookies

   ○ a can of soup

   ○ an ice cream cone

   ○ a tennis ball

4. Which number do the blocks shown below represent?

   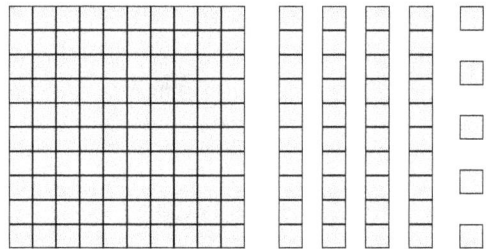

   ○ 245

   ○ 115

   ○ 145

   ○ 415

Mixed Math Skills

Test #7: Multiple Choice

5. Which shape matches the following description?

   all sides equal; all angles 90°

   ○ pentagon
   ○ square
   ○ triangle
   ○ kite

6. What value does the 5 represent in the number 3845?

   ○ 5 ones
   ○ 5 hundreds
   ○ 5 thousands
   ○ 5 tens

7. It's 10:50 in the morning. Jamal has been jogging for 25 minutes. What time did Jamal start?

   ○ 10:20 a.m.
   ○ 10:15 a.m.
   ○ 10:25 a.m.
   ○ 10:00 a.m.

8. Using the numbers 7, 5, and 9, what is the smallest and largest 3-digit number you can make? Use each number only once.

	Smallest	**Largest**
○	759	795
○	579	957
○	597	975
○	579	975

Test #7: Open Response

Mixed Math Skills

9. The chart below shows how many people came to the new pizza restaurant in its first week. Based on the pattern shown below, how many people showed up on the seventh day?

Days	1st	2nd	3rd	4th	5th	6th	7th
Number of People	12	14	26	40	66	106	

Show your work.

_____ people showed up on the 7th day.

10. Brittney was almost done with a painting of her dog. She scheduled the following times to complete her work over the next three days.

   Day 1: 10:20 to 10:45

   Day 2: 11:45 to 12:30

   Day 3: 9:00 to 9:30

   How many minutes did she spend painting each day?

   Day 1: _____ minutes

   Day 2: _____ minutes

   Day 3: _____ minutes

Mixed Math Skills

11. Write the numbers in the box below in the correct part of the Venn-diagram. Show the numbers that can be divided by 2 on the left, show the numbers that can be divided by 5 on the right. In the place where the circles overlap, show which numbers can be divided by **both** 2 and 5.

8, 16, 15, 20, 36, 45, 70, 80, 72, 10, 28, 60, 105, 14

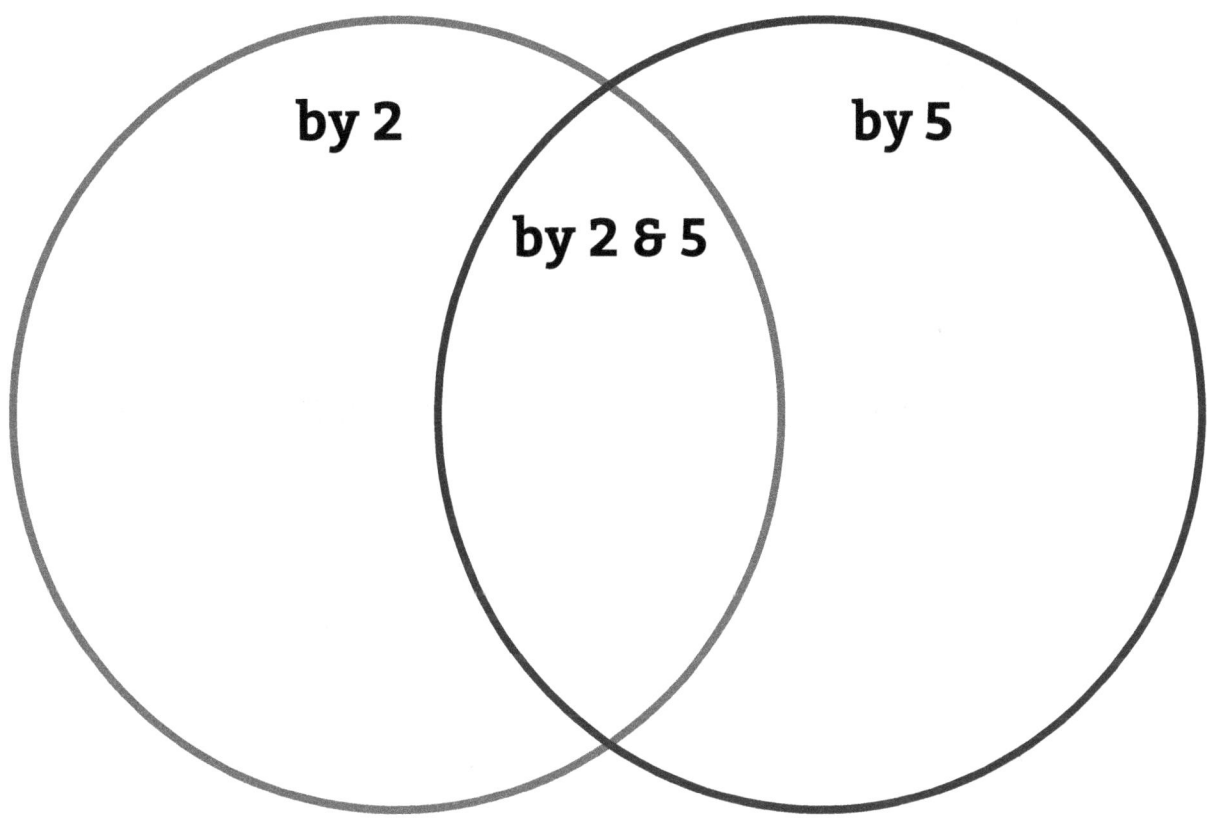

Justify your answers.

Test #7: Open Response

Mixed Math Skills

12. Each of the square units on the grids below represent a dollar amount.

    On Grid A, it takes $25.00 to fill ½ unit. Shade in the correct number of units to represent $300.00.

    On Grid B, it takes $20.00 to fill ½ unit. Shade in the correct number of units to represent $200.00.

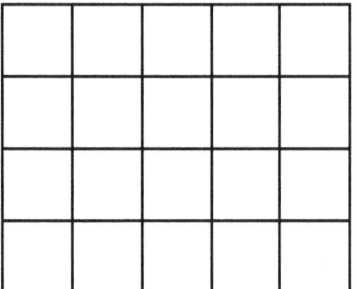
Grid A

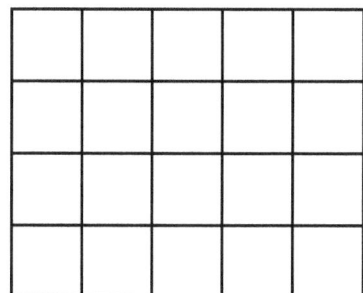
Grid B

Show your work. Justify your answer.

_____ **units represent $300.00**

_____ **units represent $200.00**

Test #7: Open Response

Mixed Math Skills

13. Mrs. Wu has 12 chickens. Each chicken lays 4 eggs each day. She gathers the eggs in 3 baskets. She puts an equal amount of eggs in each basket.

   a. How many eggs per basket?

   b. If one of the chickens lays only 1 egg, how many eggs per basket?

Show your work. Justify your answer.

   a. There are _____ eggs in each basket.

   b. There are _____ eggs in each basket

Test #7: Open Response

Mixed Math Skills

14. Mr. Anderson has 8 learning centres in 3 different categories in his classroom. Each school day, Mr. Anderson chooses 3 centres for the students to work in.

Subject Centres	Media Centres	Creative Centres
Science	Computers	Art
Writing	Listening	Theatre
Reading	Magazines	

How many different combinations of centres can Mr. Anderson have?

Show all the possible combinations on this calendar for the month of October.

Use the first letter of each centre as a symbol to record your combinations.

SUN.	MON.	TUES.	WED.	THURS.	FRI.	SAT.
	1	2	3	4	5	6
7	8	9	10	11	12	13
14	15	16	17	18	19	20
21	22	23	24	25	26	27
28	29	30	31			

There are _____ combinations possible.

Mixed Math Skills

Test #7: Multiple Choice

15. There are 30 students in the class. If a litre of water can fill 5 glasses, how many litres will it take to give each student a glass of water.

    ○ 4 litres

    ○ 1 litre

    ○ 6 litres

    ○ 30 litres

16. Jonah has $36.00. He gave each of his friends $3.00 and he had $3.00 left.

    How many friends did Jonah give money to?

    ○ 12 friends

    ○ 10 friends

    ○ 11 friends

    ○ 9 friends

17. How many grams in a kilogram?

    ○ 100 grams

    ○ 1000 grams

    ○ 10 grams

    ○ 200 grams

18. Which number completes the following number sentence?

    8 x 3 + 5 + 6 – ☐ = 32

    ○ 3

    ○ 2

    ○ 5

    ○ 4

Test #8: Multiple Choice

Mixed Math Skills

1. The animal shelter has 10 white kitties, 6 calico kitties, 4 orange striped kitties and 1 grey kitty ready to be adopted.

   Which word best describes the chance that a black kitty will be adopted?

   ○ unlikely
   ○ certain
   ○ likely
   ○ impossible

2. What is the smallest 3-digit number you can make from the 5 numbers below? Use each number only once.

   3 8 4 1 6

   ○ 641
   ○ 134
   ○ 168
   ○ 341

3. Which pair of numbers has the sum of 220?

   ○ 158   62
   ○ 115   181
   ○ 89   116
   ○ 110   140

4. Which of the following shapes is a tetrahedron?

   ○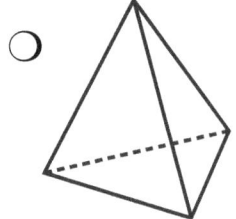

   ○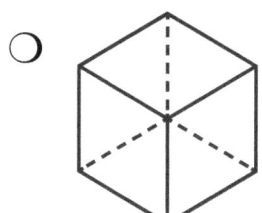

   ○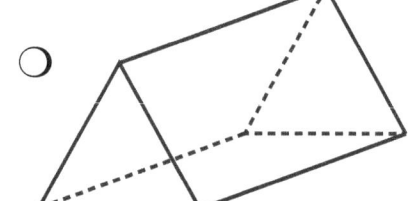

   ○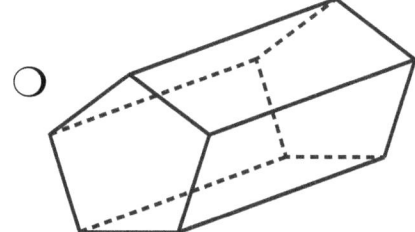

Mixed Math Skills

Test #8: Multiple Choice

5. Mr. Lynch's third grade class did a survey to find out what the most common names were in the school. The chart below shows the number of students with the top boy and girl names.

BOYS	GIRLS
Liam = 12	Olivia = 15
William = 19	Maya = 18
Jacob = 13	Sofia = 12
Lucas = 18	Emma = 15
Ben = 14	Sara = 18

What number shows the mode of the data?

○ 12
○ 18
○ 15
○ 13

6. Which thermometer shows 8°C?

○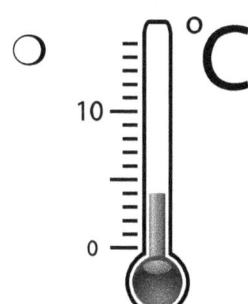

○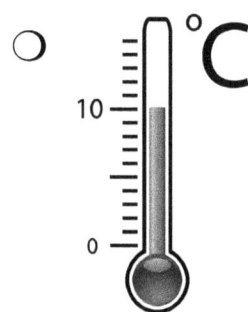

○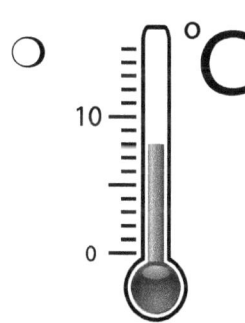

○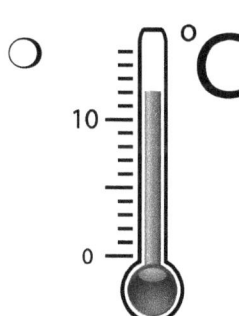

Mixed Math Skills

Test #8: Multiple Choice

7. Niveta has the amount of money shown below to buy a hat that cost $12.75.

Which set of coins shows how much more money Niveta will need to buy the hat?

○

○

○

○

8. Which of the following shapes are congruent?

1. 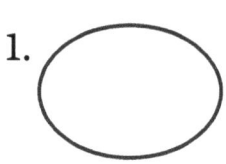   2.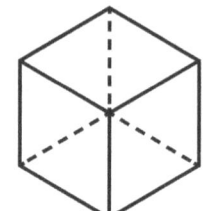

3. 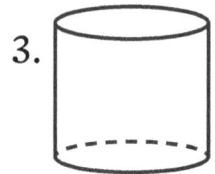   4.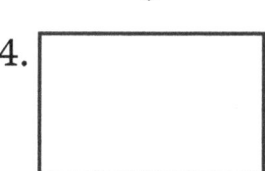

5. 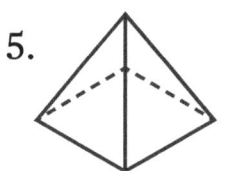 6.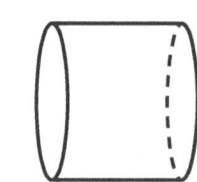

7. 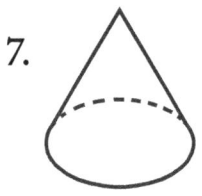 8.

9. 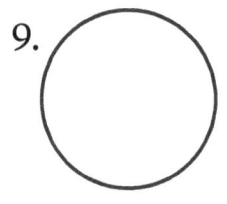 10.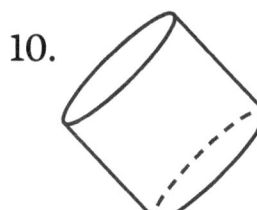

○ 1, 7, 9

○ 8, 5, 2

○ 3, 6, 10

○ 9, 3, 1

Mixed Math Skills

Test #8: Multiple Choice

9. Andy uses popsicle sticks to create the pattern below.

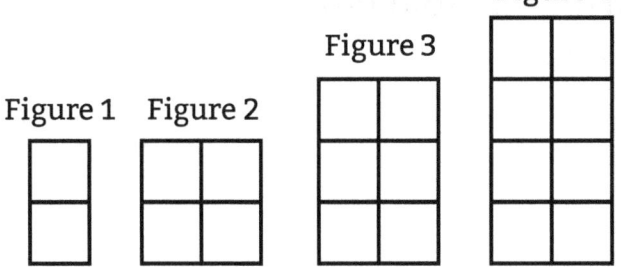

   What number pattern describes the number of popsicles sticks that Andy uses?

   ○ 2, 4, 6, 8
   ○ 4, 8, 12, 16
   ○ 7, 12, 17, 22
   ○ 7, 14, 21, 28

10. How many rows of dots in groups of 4 must you count in order to get 24 dots?

    ○ 4
    ○ 6
    ○ 5
    ○ 2

11. The pictograph below shows the number of trees members of the forest service planted in one month.

Name	Trees Planted
Josh	🌲🌲🌲🌲🌲
Andrea	🌲🌲🌲🌲🌲🌲
Luke	🌲🌲🌲🌲
Justin	🌲🌲🌲🌲🌲🌲🌲🌲🌲

    Each 🌲 = 4 trees

    Which person planted 36 trees?

    ○ Josh
    ○ Andrea
    ○ Luke
    ○ Justin

Test #8: Open Response

Mixed Math Skills

12. Bailey is in the Girl Guides and sells cookies each year to help raise money. Each box of cookies cost $5.00. In the fall she sold 56 boxes of chocolaty mint cookies. In the spring she sold boxes of chocolate sandwich and vanilla sandwich cookies.

    She sold ¼ as many boxes of vanilla sandwich cookies as chocolaty mint cookies.

    How many boxes of vanilla sandwich cookies did she sell?

    She sold ½ as many boxes of chocolate sandwich cookies as chocolaty mint cookies.

    How many boxes of chocolate sandwich cookies did she sell?

    How much more money did she make selling chocolaty mint cookies than the chocolate sandwich cookies?

Show your work.

Bailey sold _____ **boxes of vanilla sandwich cookies.**

Bailey sold _____ **boxes of chocolate sandwich cookies.**

Bailey made _____ **more selling chocolaty mint cookies.**

Test #8: Open Response

Mixed Math Skills

13. Coach Riley has 18 basketballs to put away after the game. Show two different ways he can arrange the basketballs in equal rows on the shelves in the storage closet.

    Write a division sentence for each way he can arrange the basketballs.

First way: Draw rows of equal lengths.

Division Sentence 1: _____

Second Way: Draw rows of equal lengths.

Division Sentence 2: _____

Test #8: Open Response

Mixed Math Skills

14. Marco shades a growing number pattern on the chart below. Marco's pattern starts with the number 4.

   Finish shading in the boxes on the chart using Marco's pattern rule.

   What is Marco's pattern rule?

   Pattern rule: _____

1	2	3	4	5
6	7	8	9	10
11	12	13	14	15
16	17	18	19	20
21	22	23	24	25
26	27	28	29	30
31	32	33	34	35
36	37	38	39	40
41	42	43	44	45
46	47	48	49	50

   Complete the following number patterns using Marco's pattern rule.

   a. 7, _____, _____, _____, _____

   b. _____, 5, _____, _____, _____

Test #8: Multiple Choice

Mixed Math Skills

15. Look at the prism below.

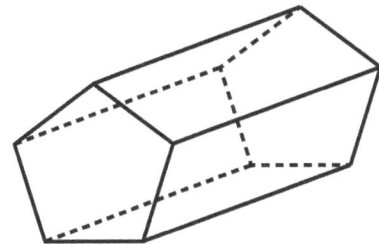

   Which of the following describes all the faces of the prism?

   ○ 5 pentagons, 2 rectangles

   ○ 2 pentagons, 5 rectangles

   ○ 2 octagons, 4 rectangles

   ○ 2 hexagons, 6 rectangles

16. Emily's puppy is 42 days old. How many weeks old is Emily's puppy?

   ○ 6 weeks

   ○ 7 weeks

   ○ 4 weeks

   ○ 5 weeks

17. Look at the number sentence below.

   34 + 22 = ☐

   Which of the following could be put in the number box to make the number sentence true?

   ○ 20 + 6 + 30

   ○ 8 + 30 + 30

   ○ 20 + 6 + 20

   ○ 30 + 20 + 5

Test #9: Multiple Choice

Mixed Math Skills

1. $12.00 plus $16.10 plus $10.30 equals

   ○ $28.50
   ○ $48.40
   ○ $38.30
   ○ $38.40

2. Each side of the squares shown in the grid below measures 1cm. What is the perimeter of the shaded in figure?

   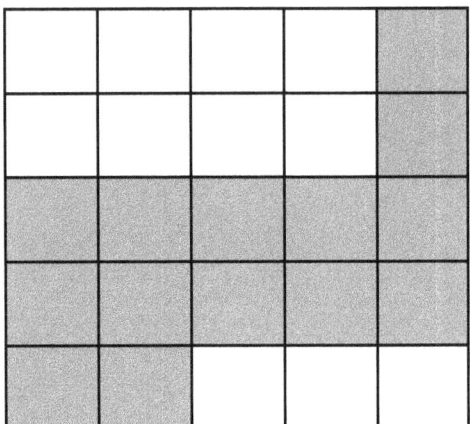

   ○ 14 cm
   ○ 19 cm
   ○ 20 cm
   ○ 18 cm

3. Which shape has 8 edges and 5 vertices?

   ○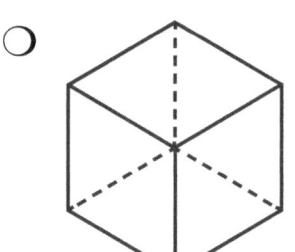

   ○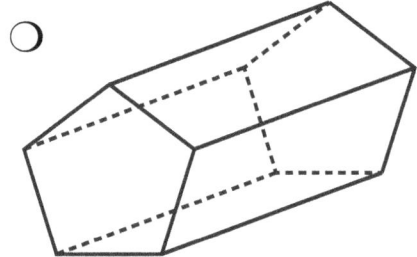

   ○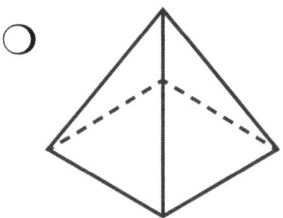

   ○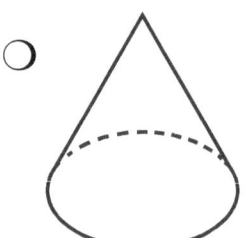

Test #9: Multiple Choice

Mixed Math Skills

4. Which number completes the following number sentence?

   $9 \times 8 - \boxed{} = 66$

   ○ 5
   ○ 8
   ○ 9
   ○ 6

5. ¼ of 12 plus 1/3 of 21 equals

   ○ 33
   ○ 14
   ○ 10
   ○ 8

6. What is the pattern rule of the following number pattern?

   15, 22, 29, 36, 43

   ○ add 7
   ○ add 5
   ○ add 6
   ○ add 8

7. Happy Time Florist sells lots of flower bouquets on Valentine's Day.

   The chart below shows how many of each kind of bouquet was sold.

Type of Flower Bouquet	Amount Sold
Roses	58
Daisies	22
Tulips	39
Lillies	44

   How many total bouquets were sold on Valentine's Day?

   ○ 160
   ○ 163
   ○ 185
   ○ 144

Test #9: Open Response

Mixed Math Skills

8. Timberland Sports is having a big sale to make room for new stock. The following items have been reduced by 1/2.

Basketball: $20.00

Tennis Racquet: $80.00

Baseball: $10.00

If you buy one of each item, how much will you save on the sale?

Show your work. Justify your answer.

I will save _____.

Test #9: Open Response

Mixed Math Skills

9. Ms. Hawkins third grade class is having a contest between the boys and the girls to see who can sell more rolls of wrapping paper to raise money for a class trip.

   The chart below shows information about how many rolls of wrapping paper were sold in two days.

Day	Number of Rolls Sold by Girls	Number of Rolls Sold by Boys
Thursday	28	19
Friday	?	29

   The total number of rolls sold over the two days is 100.

   How many rolls did the girls sell on Friday?

   Who won the contest – the boys or the girls?

   Show your work.

   The girls sold _____ rolls on Friday.

   The _____ won the contest.

Test #9: Open Response

Mixed Math Skills

10. The chart below shows icons that represent faces, flowers, and shapes.

	Faces	Flowers	Shapes
1	☺	✿	■
2	☹	❀	●
3	😐	❋	◆

How many different combinations can you make with these icons?

Show your work. You can assign a letter to represent each icon to make your calculations easier.

I can make _____ different combinations.

Mixed Math Skills

Test #9: Multiple Choice

11. Which of these groups has 6 more hearts than stars?

   ○ ♥♥♥♥★★★★★★
   ○ ♥♥♥♥♥★★★★
   ○ ♥♥♥♥♥♥♥★
   ○ ♥★★★★★★★

12. Sam earns $500.00 per week at his job. What else do you need to know to find out how much Sam earns in a day?

   ○ How many hours Sam works in a day.
   ○ How many days Sam works in a week.
   ○ How much Sam makes an hour.
   ○ How much Sam makes in a year.

13. How many of Shape A were needed to make Shape B?

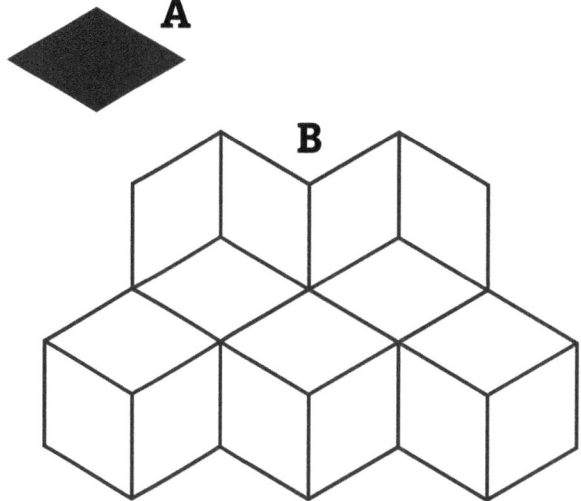

   ○ 10
   ○ 15
   ○ 20
   ○ 12

Mixed Math Skills

Test #9: Multiple Choice

14. Which combination of coins equals $4.85?

○

○

○

○

15. Sanjay is at the movie with his friend. It is 9:15. The movie has been playing for 75 minutes.

   Which clock below shows what time the movie started?

○

○

○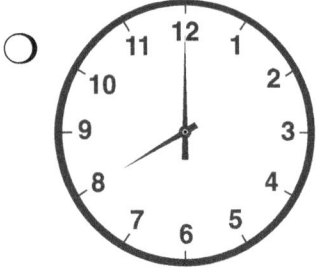

○

Test #9: Open Response

Mixed Math Skills

16. The pictograph below shows loaded freight cars in the railroad yard. Each set of freight cars is on a different rail line. Each freight car holds 500 boxes.

Railroad Line	Number of Freight Cars
Line 1	🚃🚃🚃🚃🚃
Line 2	🚃🚃🚃
Line 3	🚃🚃🚃🚃🚃🚃🚃🚃
Line 4	🚃🚃
Line 5	

a. Which Rail Line shows the number of freight cars needed to hold 1500 boxes?

b. There are 2500 boxes that still need to be loaded for Rail Line 5. How many freight cars will be needed?

Show your work.

a. Rail Line _____ shows how many freight cars are needed.

b. _____ freight cars will be needed.

Test #10: Multiple Choice

Mixed Math Skills

1. Which of the following sets of blocks represents the number 185?

   ○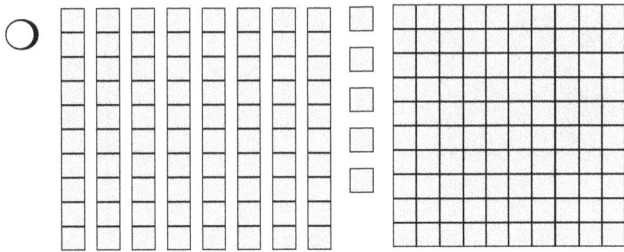

   ○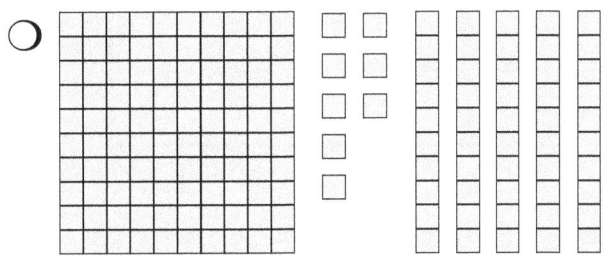

   ○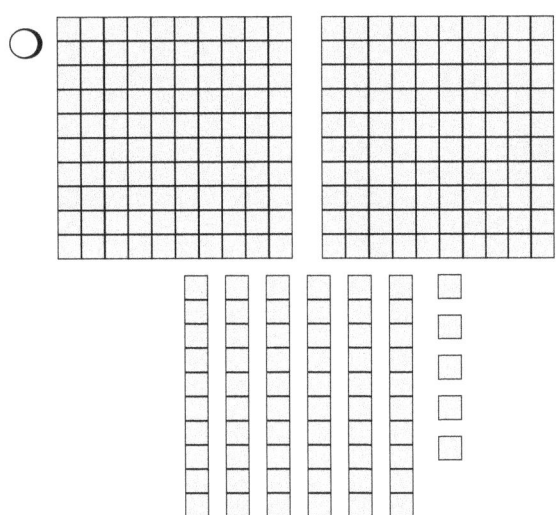

   ○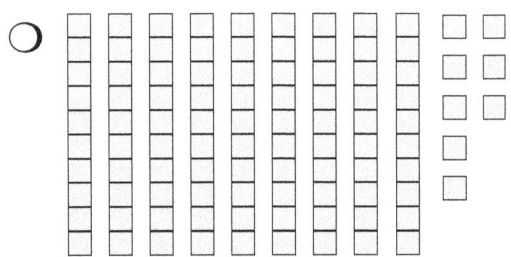

2. Mrs. Gupta bought a pair of mittens and a scarf with the coins shown below.

   Gloves   **Scarf**

   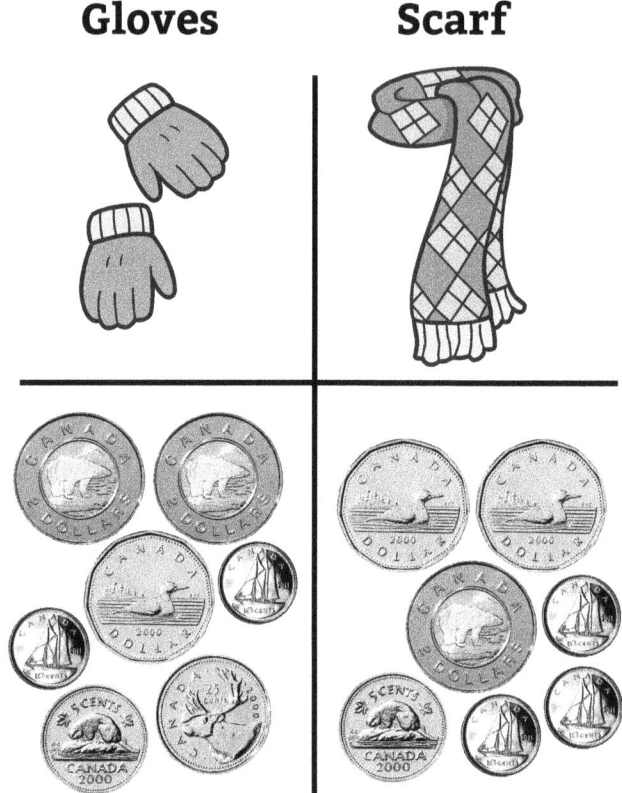

   How much did she spend on these two items?

   ○ $10.25

   ○ $9.85

   ○ $8.75

   ○ $9.90

Mixed Math Skills

Test #10: Open Response

3. Mira's favorite TV show is on between 7:00 and 8:00 in the evening.

    There are 4 commercial breaks during her show. The first break lasts 4 minutes, the second break lasts 5 minutes, the third and fourth breaks last 3 minutes each.

    How many minutes of her show does Mira actually get to see?

    Show your work. Justify your answer.

    Mira gets to see _____ minutes of her show.

Test #10: Multiple Choice

Mixed Math Skills

4. What value does the 5 represent in the number 4583?

   ○ 5 hundreds

   ○ 5 thousands

   ○ 5 ones

   ○ 5 tens

5. The arrow has gone through two transformations. Which of the following two words describes those transformations?

   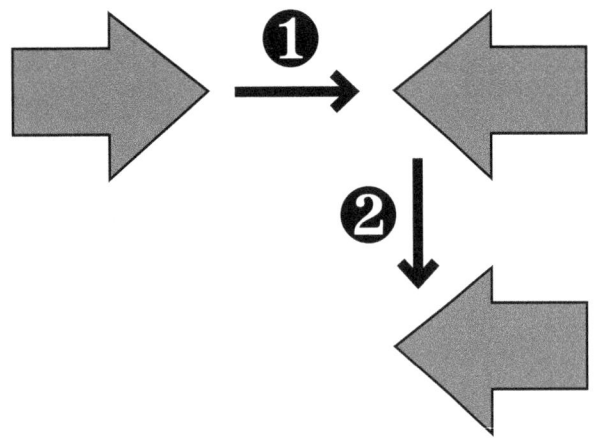

   ○ rotation, reflection

   ○ reflection, reflection

   ○ reflection, translation

   ○ translation, rotation

6. Using the numbers 4, 2, and 8, what is the smallest and the largest 3-digit number you can make? Use each number only once.

	Smallest	Largest
○	482	824
○	248	482
○	428	824
○	248	842

Mixed Math Skills

7. Look at the series of numbers in the box. Determine the pattern of the numbers.

    46, 48, 47, 49, 48, 50, ...

    Which of the numbers below comes next?

    ○ 49
    ○ 51
    ○ 50
    ○ 52

8. Which number completes the following number sentence?

    68 + 28 + 10 − 12 − 11 = ☐

    ○ 77
    ○ 78
    ○ 83
    ○ 98

9. Marsha and Robin are going on a road trip. It will take them 3 days to get to the lake. How many hours will it take?

    ○ 96 hours
    ○ 24 hours
    ○ 48 hours
    ○ 72 hours

10. Which of the following items are measured in kilograms?

    ○ sofa, table
    ○ pears, potatoes
    ○ pencil, eraser
    ○ photo album, basketball

Mixed Math Skills

Test #10: Open Response

11. Each square equals 1 unit. What is the area of each of the shapes shown in the grid below?

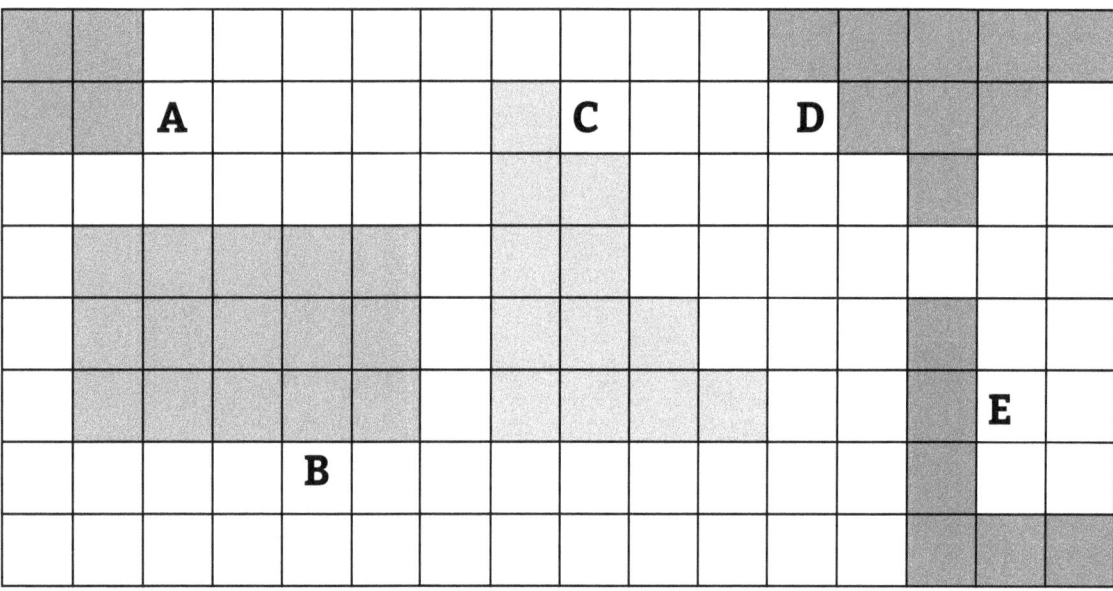

The area of Shape A is _____ units.

The area of Shape B is _____ units.

The area of Shape C is _____ units.

The area of Shape D is _____ units.

The area of Shape E is _____ units.

Mixed Math Skills

12. There are 100 nails in each box. If Seth uses 834 nails for his project, how many boxes will he need?

    ○ 5 boxes

    ○ 3 boxes

    ○ 9 boxes

    ○ 7 boxes

13. One year is equal to how many weeks?

    ○ 365 weeks

    ○ 150 weeks

    ○ 1000 weeks

    ○ 52 weeks

14. If you count by tens, what is the value of the second Y in the figure below?

    • Y • • • Y • • • • •

    ○ 30

    ○ 50

    ○ 60

    ○ 90

15. Which of the following can be measured in kilometres?

    ○ the height of a house

    ○ the length of a block

    ○ the distance from Toronto to Ottawa

    ○ the size of a bed

Mixed Math Skills

Test #10: Open Response

16. How would you express the following amounts of money in dollars and cents?

   990 cents = _____   407 cents = _____

   100 cents = _____   1200 cents = _____

   > Show your work.

17. How many 25¢ coins in ½ of $1.00? How many 25¢ coins in ¼ of $1.00? How many 25¢ coins in ¾ of $1.00?

   > Show your work.
   >
   > ____ 25¢ coins in ½   ____ 25¢ coins in ¼   ____ 25¢ coins in ¾

Mixed Math Skills

Test #10: Multiple Choice

18. ½ of 16 plus ½ of 28 equals

   ○ 25
   ○ 22
   ○ 30
   ○ 32

19. Which pair of numbers complete the following number sentences.

   a. 8 x 5 = 55 – ☐

   b. 9 + 6 + 3 – ☐ = 12

   ○ a. 10   b. 8
   ○ a. 15   b. 6
   ○ a. 12   b. 5
   ○ a. 14   b. 4

20. If the temperature in Toronto is 27°C, what time of year is it most likely to be?

   ○ winter
   ○ summer
   ○ spring
   ○ fall

21. If you added 2 decimetres to 55 centimetres, how many centimetres would you have?

   ○ 57 centemetres
   ○ 75 centemetres
   ○ 110 centemetres
   ○ 65 centemetres

Answer Key

TEST #1: NUMBER SENSE AND NUMERATION
1. 129
2. 50, 75, 100, 125
3. 5, 8, 4
4. 37 + 39 = 76
5. 6 hundreds
6. 26
7. 2301   2310   2321
8.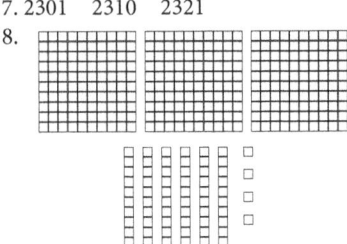
9. 55, 13
10. 11
11. 300
12. 49   11
13. 3 thousands and 8 ones
14. $6.50 $4.50
15. 16 ÷ 2 = 8
16. 8432
17. 10

TEST #2: PATTERNING AND ALGEBRA
1. 46
2. 16
3. ✶✶   ✶✶✶✶   ✶✶✶✶✶✶
4. 3 x 6 + 6 = 24
5. a. 56, 72, 88   b. 16, 12, 8   c. 60, 24, 12
6. a. 2   b. 56   c. 5
7. 8 0 4
8. a. 16, 32, 64, 128   b. 25, 28, 31, 34   c. JI, LK, NM, PO
9. 8
10. shaded numbers row 6: 52, 58
    shaded numbers row 7: 64, 70
    shaded number row 8: 76
    shaded numbers row 9: 82, 88
    shaded numbers row 10: 94, 100
    a. 50   b. 134   c. 194
11. 629, 624, 619, 614
12. shape and number
13. 6 x 8 = 48
14. going to the movies every Friday
15. 359, 350, 347
16. 28
17. add 4
18. 4 x 8 = 32   32 ÷ 4 = 8
19. 11 students

TEST #3: MEASUREMENT
1.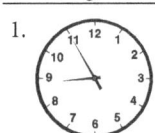
2. kilometre
3.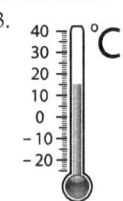
4. 180
5. recess
6. 5:10
7.
8. gasoline, milk
9. 72
10. 10:20
11. 4 bottles
12. 18 cm
13. 17 squares
14. ¼ litre
15. horse pasture
16. 15, 150
17. Plan A

TEST #4: GEOMETRY AND SPATIAL SENSE
1. square-based pyramid
2. 8 sides
3. rectangle
4. cone
5. cylinder
6. X
7. 6 shapes
8. rectangle
9.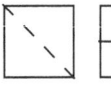
10. 4, 6, 10
11. 3 k down, 8 k to the left
    3 k down, 5 k to the right
    3 k to the right, 6 k up
12. b, d, e, f   a, c, g, h
13.

Answer Key

14. reflection, rotation
15. 9 edges, 6 vertices
16. triangle
17. rectangular prism
18. rhombus

TEST #5: DATA MANAGEMENT AND PROBABILITY

1. 1 chance out of 4
2. 32
3. 8
4. certain, unlikely, likely, likely, impossible, certain
5. brown horse, donkey, black horse, white horse
6. 90, Spinner B
7. 103, 8, 117
8. ☺☺☺; comedy
9. 2 out of 6
10. likely
11. There were three more rainy days than sunny days.
12. 4

TEST #6: MIXED MATH SKILLS

1. 5 + 5 + 5 + 5=
2. ———•——•——•——•——•——•——
       15   25 30   40   45
3. 3
4. 18 more cows
5. four combinations
6. 26, 30, 34
7. cube
8. 18
9. $2.00
10. 4 lines of symmetry
11.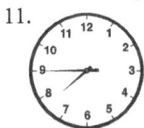
12. 9, $27.00
13.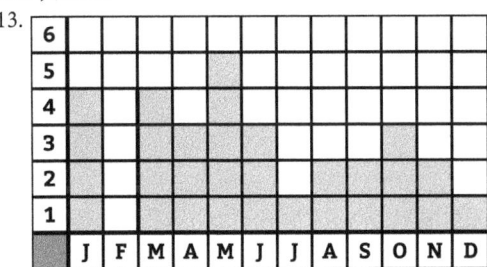
30, 4, April, May, June, July, October, December
14. 3 out of 8
15. rotation
16. centimetre
17. -3°C
18. 32 sides, 37 squares, the area is greater
19. Day 6
20. $12.00

TEST #7: MIXED MATH SKILLS

1. subtract 3
2. 27 ÷ 9 = 3
3. a can of soup
4. 145
5. square
6. 5 ones
7. 10:25 a.m.
8. 579, 975
9. 172
10. 25 minutes, 45 minutes, 30 minutes
11. by 2: 8, 10, 14, 16, 20, 28, 36, 60, 70, 72, 80
    by 5: 10, 15, 20, 45, 60, 70, 80, 105
    by 2 & 5: 10, 20, 60, 70, 80
12. 6, 5
13. 16, 15
14. 18
15. 6 litres
16. 11 friends
17. 1000 grams
18. 3

TEST #8: MIXED MATH SKILLS

1. impossible
2. 134
3. 158 62
4.
5. 18
6.
7. $2 coin, 4 quarters, 2 dimes, 1 nickel
8. 3, 6, 10
9. 7, 12, 17, 22
10. 6
11. Justin
12. 14, 28, $140
13. 18 ÷ 2 = 9   18 ÷ 3 = 6
14. add 3   a. 10, 13, 16, 19   b. 2, 8, 11, 14
15. 2 pentagons, 5 rectangles
16. 6 weeks
17. 20 + 6 + 30

TEST #9: MIXED MATH SKILLS

1. $38.40
2. 19 cm
3. square based pyramid
4. 6
5. 10
6. add 7

7. 163
8. $55.00
9. 24, girls
10. 27
11. ♥ ♥ ♥ ♥ ♥ ♥ ♥ ★
12. How many days Sam works in a week.
13. 15
14. $2 coin, $1 coin, 4 quarters, 6 dimes, 5 nickels
15. 8:00
16. Rail Line 2, 5

TEST #10: MIXED MATH SKILLS

1.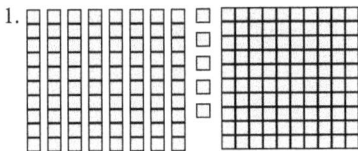
2. $9.85
3. 45 minutes
4. 5 hundreds
5. reflection, translation
6. 248, 842
7. 49
8. 83
9. 72 hours
10. pears, potatoes
11. Shape: A 4   B 15,   C 12   D 9, E 6
12. 9 boxes
13. 52 weeks
14. 50
15. the distance from Toronto to Ottawa
16. $9.90, $4.07, $1.00, $12.00
17. 2, 1, 3
18. 22
19. a. 15   b. 6
20. summer
21. 75 centimetres

www.ingramcontent.com/pod-product-compliance
Lightning Source LLC
Chambersburg PA
CBHW062133160426
43191CB00013B/2284